# Guide To Selling Hot Sauce at a Farmer's Market

## Pocket Companion

# Thomas Robert Thompson

**Guide to Selling Hot Sauce at a Farmer's Market**

Written and Designed by Thomas Robert Thompson

Made in the Rochester NY, USA

Acknowledgments

Thanks to everyone who enjoys hot sauce and has the entrepreneurial spirt to make this book happen. Stay spicy my friends!

# Table of contents

# Section 1

# Introduction

*Farmer's markets are a great introduction to the hot sauce business with low startup costs and high profit potential*

## Why sell hot sauce at a farmer's market?

If you have purchased this book or have picked it up somewhere along the way and are reading it, you must have some interest in selling hot sauce or spicy food at a farmer's market but what was it that allured you to this business model? Many entrepreneurs in the hot sauce business may decide to sell hot sauce or spicy foods at a farm market for the following reasons.

1. **People love hot sauce**
2. **A hot sauce business is easy to start**
3. **The hot sauce market is growing**
4. **Farmer's markets are an easy startup**

1) Hot sauce and spicy foods have been getting consumed for centuries or longer and this desire is only increasing. New sauces are being created that use gourmet ingredients outside of the realm of typical hot sauces and this attracts a wide range of consumers as well as avid hot sauce customers.

2) Hot sauce recipes can consist of nothing more than blended hot peppers mixed with vinegar, water, citrus juice, or other liquids and neither of these ingredients

are very expensive. A bottle of hot sauce can be made for well under $2.00 and sold for $12.00 to $15.00 a bottle. In many states this product can be bottled in a home kitchen and sold directly to consumers under local cottage food laws with an investment of nothing more than raw goods.

Therefore, easy accessibility to a product that sells for a high profit margin with little startup costs is a business model that is easy to start.

3) The demand for hot sauce by consumers is growing and so is their acceptance to try new products on the market. The hot sauce market has reached Generation Z and these consumers are growing up enjoying hot sauce. In addition, ethnic cultures who consume hot sauce and spicy foods as a regular part of their meals are growing. Indian, Asian, and Mexican populations are growing in the US, and this has and will continue to contribute to the growth of the hot sauce industry.

4) Selling hot sauce and spicy food at a farmer's market is an easy startup business model once you have a product to sell. Local markets are plentiful and the consumers that shop there are usually looking for fresh and new products that stand out among giant grocery store name brand products.

## Difference between hot sauce and spices

The difference between selling hot sauce or dried spices at a farmer's market is the shelf stability of the product. Most jurisdictions will approve dried spices over hot sauce but if your product can demonstrate shelf stability, a pH below 4.6, or a product that can demonstrate "non-potentially" hazardous methods of production, then that will improve the chances of it getting approved though local cottage food laws.

## Introduction

If you want to sell hot sauce at a farmer's market in a state that does not allow the sale of homemade hot sauce directly to consumers, then you need to follow FDA guidelines.

What this means is that the facility where you

make sauce needs to pass federal regulations through careful application processes and approval.

For many, selling hot sauce at a farmer's market means bypassing all the strict federal regulations, making homemade hot sauce, and selling it directly to consumers at a market.

However, this still means that your product, in this case hot sauce or spicy food, needs to be passed as a cottage food through the local jurisdiction where you intended to sell. In many states, about half, hot sauce is approved as a cottage food.

Hot sauce is becoming widely accepted as a cottage food in many states but there are still only about half that consider it to be safe enough for consumption and not needing strict federal inspections.

If you follow FDA regulations when bottling your hot sauce, it still may not be approved for sale directly to consumers through local farm markets because these local guidelines can be different. **However, if your hot sauce product is approved for sale under FDA regulations, it will most likely pass local regulations also.**

## Why is selling at farm markets different?

Selling hot sauce at a farmer's market is much different than selling at a physical store, online retailers, or other sales methods. **Farm markets are run by small, local organizations who want to deliver fresh, homemade, and locally made goods directly to consumers.** This helps the local economy and provides an opportunity to allow small, independent producers of food products to start up business easily. Therefore, a homemade hot sauce or dried spice made with locally grown ingredients is a welcome product at most farm markets.

Farmer's markets are usually considered an entry level introduction to the hot sauce industry. The cost of applying for permits and setting up a temporary location point to make sales can be very low. The only negative side of farmer's markets is that there may not be as many opportunities to sell hot sauce as there may be selling in stores.

**However, if you intend on selling spices, dried peppers, or spicy jams then that will broaden the opportunity for approval under cottage laws.**

## Entry level sales opportunity

Selling hot sauce at a farmer's market is an excellent entry level opportunity to enter the business. Customers are drawn to farmer's markets for the unique, artisan, and homemade products available.

Because hot sauce has caught on in the culinary and condiment world, it too has also become a widely sought after product.

## Low startup cost

The costs associated with selling hot sauce at a farmers' market usually only includes a permit fee to set up a temporary point of sales and the equipment needed to conduct sales transactions.

However, this does not include the costs associated with producing enough hot sauce to sell to consumers. Hot sauce as a product can be a very low cost to produce, making it an all-around great startup venture.

## Cost

| Manufacturing | ☐☐☐☐☐☐☐☐☐☐☐☐☐☐☐ |
|---|---|
| Product | ☐☐☐☐☐☐☐☐☐☐☐☐☐☐☐☐ |
| Permit fees | ☐☐☐☐ |
| Set up | ☐☐☐ |
| Point of sales | ☐☐☐☐ |
| Trucking | ☐☐☐☐☐☐☐ |
| Other | ☐☐ |

### How many farmer's markets are there?

Collectively in the United States there are about 9,000 farm markets, or opportunities to sell homemade hot sauce and this number continues to grow. The number of markets in each state varies but is roughly associated with the number of people residing in the areas where markets are held.

### How to find a farmer's market

If you don't already have a farm market located that you would like to sell hot sauce or spicy food at you can search any of the following

11

database.

Sometimes you can find local markets by contacting local producers of home-grown produce (farmers). Check out these great sites to find farmer's markets near you.

**Localharvest.org**

**USDA.org**

**Usdalocalfoodportal.com**

**American Farmland Trust**

**Markets.farmland.org**

**Unitedinfood.org**

**Alternatives to farmer's markets**

In many locations a farmer's market can mean freshly grown produce and crops and not so many homemade food-based products. It can also be a generic title to include any type of hand crafted and homemade products. **The regulations to sell hot sauce, spices or spicy food at an alternate location will be the same as selling at a farmer's market.** However, the flow of traffic or potential customers will be much different.

## Farm stand

A farm stand is generally set up at a roadside location and is usually a sole proprietorship selling their homegrown goods. Selling hot sauce or spices at a farm stand will follow the same regulations that farmers markets do.

There are some advantages to setting up a stand at your residence including no permit fees, controlled hours and the profit associated with being the sole proprietorship of a farm stand.

## Flea market

Flea markets are often much like a garage sale with many vendors offering products or supplies. These types of markets are not always food based but they provide a flow of traffic interested in buying unique items.

## Craft sale

Craft fairs will usually offer "homemade" or hand-crafted products but don't always place emphasis on food products like hot sauce or dried spices. However, a product that demonstrates a "craft" approach to processing could fit right in but will most likely need approval from the jurisdiction running the craft fair.

## Festivals

Festivals associated with food, food products, or hot sauce are all excellent opportunities to sell hot sauce. The only negative side to selling at a hot sauce festival is that there will be a lot of competition trying to do the same thing that you are.

### 3 things to know

As you decide to sell your homemade hot sauce at a farmer's market there are three things you should know:

1. **Do you live in a state that approves the sale of homemade hot sauce under their local cottage food laws?**

2. **Who is the contact for the local cottage food authority or person running the local farmer's market?**

3. **What are the next steps to take to get your homemade hot sauce in the hands of paying customers at a farmer's market?**

**Is hot sauce approved as a cottage food in your home state?**

Knowing if hot sauce is approved under the

cottage food laws in the state where you intend to sell will guide many other decisions. Finding this information may take several phone calls or emails to your <u>local health department or farm market coalition</u> to get direct confirmation.

**Only about half of the states in the US allow homemade hot sauce to be sold directly to consumers under local cottage food laws but those numbers are always growing.**

Knowing the local cottage food laws in your area also determines if you will need to follow FDA guidelines or not. It is in the best interest of many who intend to sell hot sauce at a farm market to avoid stringent FDA regulations.

Neither following local state regulations or federal guidelines will make a difference in how you market or sell a hot sauce at a farmer's market.

**Who to contact to verify?**

Contact the local authority on cottage food laws such as the Department of Health or Department of Agriculture in your home state. This can be a difficult thing to find but we have provided contact information for you in section 3 to get started.

Any Coalition of Farm Markets, Farmer's Market Association or Farm Market Bureau in any state should be able to provide you with a list of approved foods. Visiting any farm market near you may also help you reach the authorities who represent the persons in charge of validating the acceptance of certain homemade foods as cottage food. Attending these markets can also help you determine what type of foods are being sold. If vendors are not selling the type of food you intend to distribute…the chances are it may be because it is not allowed.

Emailing or calling someone who is the authority on the local cottage laws is only one of the many steps to follow any regulations you need to follow.

**Where to start?**

Selling hot sauce at a farm market may not begin with having a hot sauce recipe like many other business models in the hot sauce industry do. **Selling hot sauce at a local farm market depends on the local authorities accepting hot sauce under their cottage food laws.** However, you should have a hot sauce recipe available or at least one that you have made so that you fully understand what the recipe consists of. This will be an important factor in whether or not your sauce is accepted under local cottage food laws.

**What are the steps to take?**

**Step 1**

**Verify with the local agricultural agency that your hot sauce can be sold under their cottage food law.**

Step one should only take action if you already have a hot sauce recipe that you feel can compete with other hot sauce products and provide an *added value* not provided by other products also on the market. Award winning hot sauce recipes are easy to achieve and can many times be easily manipulated from existing recipes.

**Step 2**

**Make a large quantity of sauce**

Being able to take a small-quantity homemade hot sauce recipe and turn it into a large enough quantity to sell to a hundred potential customers at a farm market is extremely important. Many times, recipes can change as the quantities are increased and the integrity of the sauce is lost.

## Step 3

### Locate the farmer's markets?

Farm markets have always been a popular place to sell freshly grown produce and other products closely associated with it. Hot sauce is increasingly becoming accepted as a cottage food in many states throughout the US. The chances are there is a farmer's market within a short distance of your home operation. Search the **world database of farm markets** to find one near you.

### Making sauce safe for consumption

The number one stipulation for states that approve hot sauce under cottage food laws is that it is **safe for consumption** or offers a shelf stable product to consumers.

Having an original hot sauce recipe is necessary for successfully selling at a farm market but may not be required for all sales opportunities. The recipe will then need to be produced to provide a safe, shelf-stable hot sauce to consumers.

This means the hot sauce needs to have a pH level of 4.6 or lower, which will be explored in section 5 and will also need to follow sanitary conditions during packaging.

## Sanitization

Providing a safe hot sauce product to consumers begins with sanitizing the equipment and bottles used during processing. This is important no matter where you are selling and is many times required by the local jurisdictions through inspections. Be prepared to have the kitchen space where you are preparing hot sauce undergo inspections for cleanliness and the proper sanitization methods.

## Sanitization methods

Sanitization methods of the equipment and packaging used to bottle hot sauce may not be as stringent as the standards on a federal level. However, sanitizing in general is important because it could directly affect the end results of the consumers product.

Some states require the manufacturer of hot sauce (you), to take safety training courses. This is to ensure that the product you intend to sell is handled properly and will not cause harm to those consuming it.

Homemade foods don't always have preservatives or use preservative methods that protect the foods like commercially available products do.

## Washing

Washing equipment and kitchen space regularly with hot soapy water is proper and can eliminate unwanted bacteria. Using hot water with a temperature of 140° F or higher with an antibacterial soap is most effective against unwanted bacteria.

## Sterilization equipment

Small appliances can be purchased that can sterilize equipment, especially if you are only bottling a few cases at a time. Many times, selling hot sauce at a farmer's market can be an entry into the hot sauce industry so you may not want to invest in expensive, commercial equipment.

## States requiring food handling safety course

| | |
|---|---|
| Alabama | Oregon |
| Illinois | Rhode Island |
| Maryland | South Dakota |
| Minnesota | Texas |
| Nevada | Utah |
| Oklahoma | Virginia |

# Section 2

# Make the Sauce

*To be accepted as a cottage food in most states, a hot sauce recipe will need to have a pH of 4.6 or lower to demonstrate shelf stability*

Sales become a person-to-person sales approach when operating at a farmer's market so presenting your product and knowing what the recipe consists of are very important. This information may also need to be presented to the local group of authoritative figures who will be approving the hot sauce for sale directly to consumers at local farm markets.

### Recipe

**The hot sauce recipe is one of the most important aspects of selling hot sauce at a farmer's market.** Unique and flavorful gourmet hot sauces will allow your product to stand out among the competition and can be one of the first aspects leading to successful sales.

### Making hot sauce

Making any type of hot sauce is a simple combination of mixing hot peppers with other ingredients and blending them.

However, some other processes used will make a difference in how the sauce tastes and appears, as well as the aroma it gives off. Many hot sauces may be simple recipes but there are four things to contemplate in making a great hot sauce that stands out among the rest.

**Four things need to be considered in making a great hot sauce to be sold at a farmer's market:**

**1) What are the ingredients used?,**

**2) What is the quantity of each ingredient?,**

**3) What is the process in which they undergo?**

**4) What type of equipment will be used in the processing.**

**Each of these elements should be separated and defined with each batch of sauce to create unique recipes distinctive of themselves.**

The secrets of a hot sauce recipe and the process in which it is made will be no "secret" to those approving your product.

**How a hot sauce is made and the processed used can directly influence its acceptance as a cottage food.**

Also keep in mind that you may need to divulge precise information to people or document trade secret processes to get your sauce approved.

The preparation and process for making hot sauce are what make the hot sauce stand out. The ingredients used to make hot sauce and the quantity of each ingredient are just as important.

Also, consider the equipment used because this can be a factor in the consistency and appearance of the hot sauce.

Very distinct hot sauces can be made by simply adjusting one or all four of the factors that go into making a hot sauce.

The combination of ingredients and processes used to make hot sauce seem endless but breaking things down into four areas can help clarify the importance of each one and how they are used in making hot sauce.

Understand and experiment with each one and make hot sauce bold in flavor and full of culinary potential.

## 1] Ingredients

Choosing the right ingredients can make or break a hot sauce recipe. For example, the first ingredient is likely the type of hot pepper. Although there are many varieties of peppers there are typically only 25 common hot peppers used in hot sauce. Many of these will have a flavor, as well as a level of heat, that will be unique to that variety. These peppers are used with other peppers or are used to highlight the individual flavors of the peppers.

Consider these questions when preparing to make hot sauce intended to be sold at a farmer's market. Are there similar sauces at the local farmer's market? Does your sauce stand out in appearance?

Color can play a role in the appearance of a hot sauce especially if you are looking to make a sauce outside of the traditional red. **Yellow, orange, and even purple hot peppers can draw the attention of the consumer**, but you still need the right combination and quantity.

A hot sauce will have more than just hot peppers. The selection of additional ingredients either within a recipe or as an additive can define its flavor. Of the 1,000's of hot sauces on the market today there are common ingredients that many of them will use. It is the combination of the selection of the ingredients that make it stand out.

## 2] Quantity

The next step in making a hot sauce would be choosing the quantity or amount of each ingredient. The best way to do this would be to **select an existing recipe with the quantities pre-determined.** A recipe cannot be copyright protected but the process in which it is made can be and this will be a huge factor in the end product of the sauce.

An additional way to determine the quantity of ingredients is to read the ingredient label of some popular hot sauces. This will give you the ratio of each ingredient against the other ingredients but not necessarily the quantity of each one. This is probably part of the trade secret for many manufacturers and a unique hot sauce recipe is what stands out, not a copycat.

The quantity of each ingredient can make or break the quality of the recipe. For example, too much water will dilute the flavor and heat of a hot pepper, the whole reason for making hot sauce, and "water it down. Also, too many ingredients such as salt, garlic, or vinegar can be overpowering. There are already ingredients that have a great level of pungency to them.

## 3] Process

The process in which a hot sauce is made is one of the most important steps in making a hot sauce and is what adds to the uniqueness of the recipe. This will make it stand out in flavor, contribute to preserving, and also provides contrast in the way a hot sauce appears.

As equal importance as appearance is the aroma of a hot sauce. The process, or lack thereof, can be vastly different from the flavor. For example, a hot sauce using smoked or roasted peppers will have a distinct aroma as well as a sauce that uses aromatic spices like garlic, basil, or cumin.

Taking three simple ingredients such as hot peppers, vinegar, and salt and putting them through three distinctly different processes will make sauces that contrast in flavor, appearance, and aroma. Most processes such as roasting, cooking, smoking, and fermenting will use completely different equipment as well.

**4] Equipment**

The number one piece of equipment that most hot sauces will use is a blender to get the smooth consistency of a sauce. Some processes such as fermenting, cooking, and roasting will break down the pepper and make blending easier, but the blender itself is still needed.

Blender wattage plays a role in the consistency of the sauce. A blender without much power or a lower speed will produce a hot sauce that is chunky in texture and may separate from liquids. A powerful blender of 900 watts or more can create a thin textured sauce typical of most hot sauce varieties.

The size of the blender will make a difference in how much sauce is made at any one time. There is some desire in the hot sauce industry for *small-batch* hot sauce, but even these marketed sauces may use commercial level equipment.

Other pieces of equipment used for cooking, roasting, or fermenting the ingredients of a hot sauce will contribute to how efficient or successful a process is, especially when the sauces are increased for mass quantities.

Study the four areas that need to be understood in making a gourmet hot sauce. Some factors may contribute to how long it takes to make a sauce or the cost of each batch. Don't let that deter you from making great gourmet hot sauces.

### Why the pH is important

**Many local cottage food laws will only allow a hot sauce to be sold if it is shelf stable or has a pH level of 4.6 or below.** In some states you will need to provide laboratory testing results similarly to FDA Regulations. Knowing the pH results from home testing will allow you to understand the acidic levels of your hot sauce but you shouldn't feel the need to attempt to lower the pH just to sell at a farm market because this could alter the recipe.

## Understanding pH

Creating hot sauce can be a science but you do not need to be a scientist to understand the importance of certain pH levels and what needs to be done to maintain it for the duration of its shelf life. Hot sauce recipes need to be tested frequently so that the pH level is known, and determined if it needs to be adjusted or not. **Many of the local cottage food laws may require laboratory testing results before a hot sauce can be considered safe to sell.**

The pH level of a hot sauce determines how long a sauce will remain fresh before and after it is opened. It is necessary to know this to understand the expiration date of a hot sauce as it applies to consumption, but this is also important for the sale at local farm markets.

**The pH of a hot sauce should be below 4.6 so the potential growth of bacteria is prohibited**, and this pH level will be consistent if states require testing results.

## What is ph?

The pH is the Potential Hydrogen that a substance has or the possibility of hydrogen ions greater than water. Depending on the level of pH in a hot sauce, it can determine the need for some adjustments to the recipe before or after it is bottled to kill harmful bacteria. Many of the products that are typically approved for sale at a farm market are not subject to harmful bacteria.

**What should the pH of hot sauce be?**

To be safe from harmful bacteria and to also avoid any complications associated with testing, a hot sauce should have a pH at or around 3.4. **There are many factors that can affect the accuracy of a reading to include the source of the ingredients, the quality of the reading device, and the temperature of the sauce at testing time.**

There is no reason to discard a hot sauce or keep from producing it if the pH is above a bacteria growth reading above 4.6. However, many states cottage food laws will not allow it to be sold directly to consumers through local markets. There are methods of bottling and packaging such as pasteurization that can lengthen the expiration date of a hot sauce if the pH is 4.6 or higher. Pasteurization is where the hot sauce is brought up to a temperature of 180° degrees for 10 minutes and then immediately bottled.

Most traditional or classic hot sauce recipes will be on the acidic side of the pH scale due to vinegar or citrus juices used in the recipes. The other side of the pH scale, above the neutrality of 7, are considered alkaline. An alkaline hot sauce can be difficult to make if you are trying to get it above 7 and can only be achieved if you leave out ingredients like vinegar and citrus. Local farm markets don't like alkaline hot sauce because homemade hot sauces may not contain preservatives to keep them fresh.

**What effects the pH?**

The level of heat or spiciness that a hot sauce has does not affect the pH level. A hot pepper with more spiciness to it does not mean that it has more acidity, or a lower level on the pH scale. Hot peppers are on the alkaline side of the scale, and this can fluctuate depending on the soil where the peppers are grown as well as the variety or species of the peppers. The amount of hot pepper contents in a hot sauce can also affect the pH but it is only because it allows more ingredients by volume that will alter the pH level.

Acidic ingredients like vinegar, lemon, lemon juice, citrus, and tomatoes will lower the pH of a hot sauce, making it more acidic. Other ingredients considered to be alkaline, mostly fruits and vegetables, will raise the pH of a hot sauce.

### Why should I test hot sauce?

Many local jurisdictions that govern the sale of homemade hot sauce require that it be pH tested before it is approved.

Anyone manufacturing hot sauce for consumption needs to know whether their sauce has the possibility of bacterial growth which can cause harm to anyone eating the sauce. The consumer also has liability if they consume sauce beyond the recommended expiration date. A homemade hot sauce, no matter what the ingredients, can last for days or weeks without harm if refrigerated. **Once sauces are manufactured and produced on a mass level for commercial sales, they need careful attention to the correct pH level through testing.**

### How often should a hot sauce be pH tested?

The pH level of a hot sauce can fluctuate for many reasons even after it has been bottled. Always test every new hot sauce creation and every batch that is made even if it is the same recipe. There are variables that can alter the pH of a hot sauce recipe that may not be noticeable with color, appearance, or flavor.

Testing should be done after a hot sauce has been both opened and unopened for any length of time after it has been bottled. Test a sauce after it has been opened at different intervals of 1 week, 2 weeks, 1 month, 3 months and 6 months. This will give a clear indication of how effective the preservation methods are. These results will be different if the hot sauce is refrigerated or not. Refrigeration slows down the ability of bacterial growth, but most hot sauce brands are not found in the refrigerated sections of grocery stores.

### How to lower the pH

The US Food and Drug Administration (FDA) states that the pH should be below 4.6 to kill potentially harmful bacteria. Some hot sauces that do not have many acidic ingredients can fall on this threshold or even higher. This means that harmful bacteria can grow in this environment and other means of lowering the pH will be needed.

### Lowering the pH without affecting flavor

One of the main ingredients of many hot sauces is vinegar. This is a very acidic ingredient that lowers the pH significantly. This is also an ingredient that has a huge influence on the flavor

33

of the hot sauce. Vinegar is not an ingredient that should be added to lower the pH after a hot sauce has been created. Some natural and synthetic preservatives can be added to create a safe pH level without altering the flavor of a hot sauce.

**How do I test pH?**

Do not guess the pH level of a hot sauce and do not dismiss it as not being important. This will determine how long a hot sauce will last in the refrigerator once it is opened as well as how long it can be stored unopened on store shelves. Knowing the expiration date of a hot sauce and providing that on a bottle of hot sauce is valuable information to both the seller and the consumer, whether you are selling at farmer's markets or grocery stores.

Testing the pH of a hot sauce can be done in a laboratory setting and probably should be conducted by these means with every new batch of hot sauce. Laboratory testing may also need to be done if a hot sauce recipe is close to an acceptable pH of 4.6 because there may be some fluctuation of this number, allowing bacterial growth.

Home meters or handheld meters are perfect for

testing every new batch of hot sauce that is created to determine the initial pH of a sauce. There are some factors that affect the accuracy of pH but having a well functioning meter can prevent some of these problems.

**Storing hot sauce**

If you mass-produce hot sauce for sale, it may not all get sold immediately at a local farm market and will have to be stored. You should not make more sauce than what your projected sales indicate, but forecasting can prove to be difficult and there may be times when you want to consider refrigerating your hot sauce to keep it fresh.

**A hot sauce does not need to be refrigerated unless it has a pH of 4.6 or higher. Most hot sauces will have a high vinegar content which will reduce the pH to a shelf-stable level below 4.6 pH. Hot sauce should be stored in room temperature conditions between 68° F (20° C) and 72° F (22° C) to ensure that it retains its potency, flavor, and freshness over time.**

**Unfortunately, many farm markets are set up outside with or without access to power so this makes refrigeration very difficult if not impossible.**

Refrigeration will take additional upfront costs for equipment and ongoing operational costs to power the equipment, refrigerator, or cooler. This will also take up space in the facility where you make hot sauce, especially if you produce it on a large scale. Fortunately, hot sauce comes in smaller containers so you can fit a lot of sauce in a standard 18 cubic foot refrigerator.

There will also be an additional cost for shipping if the sauce needs to be refrigerated during delivery. Typically, only sauces containing dairy products like cheese, cream, or milk would need consistent refrigerated delivery and storage, and these ingredients are unusual in a hot sauce.

**Storing hot sauce in the refrigerator**

If you have the room in a refrigerator or a refrigerated cooler, then there is no reason not to store hot sauce in these conditions, but most hot sauces don't need to. This will keep the flavor of the hot sauce consistent with the original recipe if a sauce needs to be stored for long durations. A refrigerator will usually have consistent temperatures and it is the inconsistent storing conditions that can influence the original flavoring of the hot sauce.

Typically, a refrigeration unit is kept at a

temperature of 40 degrees Fahrenheit or 4 degrees Celsius. Bacterial growth that creates food poisoning grows at temperatures above 45 degrees Fahrenheit.

It is important to test hot sauce for pH level throughout long storage and varying temperature conditions to ensure it will maintain its flavor and heat level.

Refrigeration is considered a form of preservation and will slow down the decay and bacterial growth of fresh foods, therefore the refrigerator or icebox was invented. However subtle it may be a hot sauce can change flavor, appearance, and heat level over time. The right stored conditions can prevent this from happening.

**What happens if a stored hot sauce gets too hot?**

**Conditions at farmers' markets are usually through the summer months when the heat and humidity is at their highest. In addition, most markets are held outside. Therefore, having products readily available and temporarily stored in hot outdoor conditions should be taken into consideration.**

Ideally, a hot sauce with a pH of 4.6 or below can be stored for long durations if temperatures are kept between 68° and 72° Fahrenheit or 20° to 22° Celsius. If these temperatures fluctuate too much, or the temperatures exceed 72 degrees for too long it can affect the contents of the hot sauce. This may be possible if a hot sauce sits outside at a farm market for lengths of time.

Any hot sauce kept or stored at temperatures above 72° F has the chance that it will "cook" and this will change the flavor, color, and heat level of the sauce. Although slow cooking temperatures are slightly above 80 degrees, long-term storage in these conditions can cause a sauce to lose its heat and pungency.

I make hot sauces that are cooked, and they become thick and rich flavorful hot sauces. However, bottled and capped hot sauces may just become gooey if stored at temperatures over 80° F (26.67° C).

**Does hot sauce go bad?**

Hot sauce will go bad…eventually. Generally speaking, it takes a period of over 6 months for hot sauce to go bad, even after it is opened. Once opened make sure the cap and top are clean and there is not any residue that has dried inside the cap or around the top of the bottle.

This could cause bacterial growth and the entire

bottle of hot sauce to go bad before its expiration date. Always check the expiration date or "best if used by" date that the manufacturer has provided on the bottle.

### How to maximize the shelf life of a hot sauce

**The shelf life of a hot sauce can be increased or extended through contents such as vinegar, citrus juices, or preservatives. However, how a sauce is stored is also important to prolong the length in which it still tastes fresh.**

Refrigeration is a preservation method but, for the cost reasons stated above, it is not typically used for hot sauces.

### Storing hot sauce long term

If you are not storing hot sauce in a refrigerator before or during delivery, then it should be stored in "room temperature" conditions until the point of sale. These conditions and temperatures can fluctuate or change within the facility that the sauce is stored but conditions should fall between 68° F (20° C) and 72° F (22° C).

What is considered the average room temperature can be different by region or by industry. For example, the pharmaceutical industry's definition of room temperature is slightly warmer than other industries.

It is safe to store hot sauce in these conditions, but the area or "room" must remain consistent with these temperatures. Regularly check and monitor temperatures and conditions of storage against the freshness of a hot sauce to ensure quality products are getting delivered. This can be done by pH testing, temperature testing, and taste testing a hot sauce over time.

**Does hot sauce lose potency over time?**

It has been my experience that hot sauces can change flavoring and the amount of heat over time. Some state that they can become hotter, less spicey, or become a "dull" flavor if not stored in the right conditions over time.

**How to tell if a hot sauce has gone bad**

You may think that it should be a no-brainer to tell if a hot sauce has gone bad or not, but some acidic vinegar-based hot sauces will take a long time to expire. Dark or black dried hot sauce on the cap or top does not necessarily mean the hot sauce has gone bad but that the residue left has dried. This is seen on most ketchup and mustard containers as well. This can cause more bacteria to grow but is not an indication the sauce has gone bad.

Hot sauce can have a strong and pungent scent to it and it can be difficult to determine if it has gone bad just by smelling it. Unlike milk which has a short shelf life and strong odor when it has expired, hot sauce is a little more subtle. If there is fuzzy-looking spotty mold growth on the surface of a hot sauce... then it has gone bad...obviously.

# Section 3

# Package the Sauce

*The labeling of a hot sauce or hot spicy product can be vastly different than sauces that are available commercially on store shelves*

## Labeling

Local farm markets do not typically have requirements for the type of bottle a hot sauce or spicy food needs to be packaged in but there are specific labeling requirements.

### Farmer's markets labeling requirements

If you want to compete with other hot sauces at farmers markets, then you need to provide a label that follows the FDA requirements. This is standard for all condiments and hot sauces, and you will see similarities just by reading the packaging.

When selling at a farmer's market, most states will also have very specific labeling requirements that indicate the product was produced without inspections or federal assessments.

When providing a label for a hot sauce or condiment the Food and Drug Administration (FDA) requires that it must include a product name, the net weight of the product, manufacturing information, and nutritional data.

The brand name and bar code are not part of the FDA label requirements. State requirements under their specific cottage food laws will be slightly varied and different in each state.

### General labeling requirements

Local state requirements may not be the same as FDA labeling requirements. You may desire to bottle and package your products with flair as if they are commercially ready for sale.

However, many consumers and shoppers at local farm markets prefer simple, natural, and clearly labeled packaging. This clarity is indicated in the state-by-state labeling requirements.

### State by state cottage food labeling requirements

### Alabama

- Name of the food
- Name of the producer or production operation
- Home or PO box address where the food was produced
- List of the ingredients in descending order of amount
- Disclaimer that the food may contain allergens

- Statement that the food is not inspected by a health department

## Alaska

- Alaska business license number
- Or name, address, and telephone number of preparer

## Arkansas

- Production date
- Name, address, and telephone number of preparer
- Product name
- Ingredients in order of predominance
- Statement - *This product was produced in a private residence that is exempt from state licensing and inspection. This product may contain allergens*

## California

- Business name and address
- Permit number
- Product name
- Ingredients
- Allergens
- Weight
- Statement - *Made in a Home Kitchen*

## Connecticut

- Name & address of operations
- Name of product
- Ingredients in order by weight
- Weight of the product
- Allergen information
- Statement - *Made in a Cottage Food Operation that is not Subject to Routine Government Food Safety Inspection*

## Delaware

- Name, phone number and email address of the cottage food producer
- Product name
- Net weight or unit count
- Production date of production
- Allergen information
- Ingredients in descending order by weight
- Statement - *This food is made in a Cottage Food Establishment and is NOT subject to routine Government Food Safety Inspections*

## Florida

- Name and address of the cottage food operation
- Name of the product

- Ingredients in descending order of predominance by weight
- Net weight or net volume
- Allergen information
- Statement - *Made in a cottage food operation that is not subject to Florida's food safety regulations*

## Georgia

- Business name and home address of the cottage food producer
- Name of the product
- Ingredients in descending order of prominence by weight
- Allergen information labeling
- Statement - *made in a cottage food operation that is not subject to state food safety inspections*

## Hawaii

- Common name of the food
- Ingredients in descending order by weight
- Producer's name and contact information
- Statement - *Made in a home kitchen not routinely inspected by the Department of Health*

47

## Idaho

- Contact information for the cottage food operation
- Allergen information
- Statement - *the food was prepared in a home kitchen not subject to regulation and inspection by any regulatory authority*

## Illinois

- Name of the cottage food operation
- The unit of local government in which the cottage food operation is located
- The identifying registration number provided by the local health department
- Name of the food product
- Ingredients listed in descending order by weight
- Date the product was processed
- Allergen information
- Statement - *This product was produced in a home kitchen not inspected by a health department that may also process common food allergens. If you have safety concerns, contact your local health department*

## Indiana

- Name and address of the person preparing the food
- Date the food was processed
- Name of the product
- Net weight and volume
- Ingredients in descending order by weight
- Statement - *This product is home produced and processed and the production area has not been inspected by the State Department of Health*

## Iowa

- Business address and business name
- Product name.
- Ingredients
- Net weight

## Kansas

- Name of the product
- Name and address of the person that made or is selling the product
- Ingredients in descending order of predominance, and quantity
- Net weight, volume, or count, depending on product

## Kentucky

- Product name
- Name and address of the homebased processing operation
- Ingredients in descending order of predominance by weight
- Net weight or volume of the product
- Production date
- Allergen warning if applicable
- Statement - *This product is home-produced and processed*

## Louisiana

- A label which clearly indicates that the food was not produced in a licensed or regulated facility

## Maine

- Maine cottage food producers do not need labels on products sold directly to consumers from home
- Products sold outside the home must include labels with product name, production address, ingredients, and product weight

## Maryland

- Name and address of the cottage food business
- Product name
- Ingredients in descending order by weight
- Net weight or volume
- Allergen information
- Nutritional information
- Statement - *Made by a cottage food business that is not subject to Maryland's food safety regulations*

## Massachusetts

- Name of the product
- Ingredients listed in descending order of predominance by weight

## Michigan

- Name and physical address of the cottage food operation
- Product name
- Ingredients in descending order of predominance by weight
- Net weight
- Allergen information

- Statement - *Made in a home kitchen that has not been inspected by the Michigan Department of Agriculture & Rural Development.* Hand-printed labels are acceptable if they are legible

## Minnesota

- Name of the producer
- Date that the food was made
- Ingredients
- Possible allergens
- Statement - *These products are homemade and not subject to state inspection*

## Mississippi

- Name and address of the cottage food operation
- Product name
- Ingredients in descending order of predominance or weight
- Net weight or volume
- Allergen information
- Nutritional information if any
- Statement - *Made in a Cottage Food operation that is not subject to Mississippi's food safety regulations*

## Missouri

- Name and address of the manufacturer

- Product name
- Ingredients in descending order of predominance
- Weight
- Statement - *Product is prepared in a kitchen that is not subject to inspection by the Missouri Department of Health and Senior Services*

## Montana

- Statement – *Food was prepared in a home kitchen*

## Nebraska

- Name and address on each package
- Statement - P*repared in a kitchen that is not subject to regulation and inspection by the regulatory authority and may contain allergens*

## New Hampshire

- Food producer's name, address, and phone number
- Product name
- Ingredients in descending order of predominance by weight
- Food allergens contained in the food

- Manufacture date, container size and product lot or batch

## New Jersey

- Product name
- Ingredients in descending order of predominance by weight
- Allergen information
- Producers name, business name, permit number, the municipality where the food was prepared
- Statement - *This food is prepared pursuant to N.J.A.C. 8:24-11 in a home kitchen that has not been inspected by the Department of Health*

## New Mexico

- Seller's contact information
- Ingredients
- Statement – *Food is home-produced and exempt from state licensing and inspection*

## New York

- Name of the product
- Ingredients in order of predominance by weight
- The total weight

- Name and address of the producer, and the producer's full address
- Any allergens statement

## North Carolina

- Label on package
- Product name
- Manufacturers name and address
- Weight in ounces / pounds
- List of ingredients by order of weight

## North Dakota

- Label statement - *This product is made in a home kitchen that is not inspected by the state or local health department*

## Ohio

- Name of the product
- Name and address of the cottage food producer's business
- Ingredients in decreasing order of prevalence by weight
- Net weight
- Statement - *This product is home produced*

## Oklahoma

- Manufacturers name and phone number
- Address where the hot sauce was produced
- Product description
- Ingredients in ascending order of proportion
- Allergen statement
- Statement - *This product was produced in a private residence that is exempt from government licensing and inspection*

## Oregon

- List of ingredients
- Weight
- Name and address of product
- Statement - *This product is homemade and is not prepared in an inspected food establishment and not for resale*

**Pennsylvania** Name of the product

- Ingredients
- Name and address of the manufacturer or distributor
- Weight
- Allergy warning, if applicable
- **Rhode Island** Ingredients
- Farm name
- Address & telephone number

## South Carolina

- Name and address of the home-based food production operation
- Product name
- Ingredients in descending order of predominance by weight
- Statement - *NOT FOR RESALE. PROCESSED AND PREPARED BY A HOME-BASED FOOD OPERATION THAT IS NOT SUBJECT TO SOUTH CAROLINA'S FOOD SAFETY REGULATIONS*

## South Dakota

- Name of the product
- Name, address, and phone number of the producer
- Date the product
- Ingredients
- Statement - *This product was not produced in a commercial kitchen. It has been home processed in a kitchen that may also process common food allergens such as tree nuts, peanuts, eggs, soy, wheat, milk, fish, and crustacean shellfish*

## Tennessee

- Name of the food
- Name and street address of the cottage food producer
- Amount of food in the package
- Ingredients in order of prominence by weight
- Lot number or date made
- Any allergens that the food contains

## Texas

- Name of food
- Name and address where food was produced
- Allergens
- **Statement -** *This food is made in a home kitchen and is not inspected by the Department of State Health Services or a local health department*

## Utah

- Name and address of business
- Product name
- Allergens
- Weight
- Statement - *This product is not for resale and was processed and prepared without state or local inspection*

## Vermont

- Name and address of the manufacturer
- Product name
- Quantity by weight
- ingredient list in descending order of predominance by weight

## Virginia

- Name, physical address, and telephone number preparer
- Date the food was processed
- Name of the product
- Weight
- List of ingredients
- Statement - *Not for resale – processed and prepared without state inspection*

## Washington

- Business name
- Permit number
- Product name
- Quantity by weight
- Ingredient list in descending order of predominance by weight

- Statement - *Made in a home kitchen that has not been subject to standard inspection criteria*

## West Virginia

- Product name
- Ingredients in descending order of predominance
- Producer's name, address, and telephone number
- Statement - *This product was produced at a private residence that is exempt from state licensing and inspection. This product may contain allergens*

## Wisconsin

- Business name and address
- Product name
- Production date
- Allergen information
- Ingredients in descending order of predominance by weight
- Statement - *This product was made in a private home not subject to state licensing or inspection*

## Wyoming
- No labeling requirements

Although many of the requirements that the Food and Drug Administration have for food products are similar to hot sauce, some nuances are specific to the type of sauce and size of the bottle. There are many versions of a hot sauce that can fall under the title of "hot sauce" so be aware of the type of sauce you have created. This is also important for marketing purposes and pairing food and both of these elements will be utilized selling hot sauce at a farmer's market. The FDA requires the type, font, or text to be bold and stand out among graphics on the label. If you are producing 5 oz bottles of sauce, which is typical, then there may not be much surface space left for the product name. Eye catching graphics may not be such a necessity and is not a typical requirement for most state cottage food laws.

**What type of sauce?**

The words "traditional" or "gourmet" do not need to accompany the words "hot sauce" but the more descriptive you are with the product the more understanding your consumers will have. The FDA does require the product name as do most state labeling requirements so if your hot sauce is more of a Picante or salsa then that needs to be included.

## Farm market hot sauce descriptions

| Artisan | All natural |
|---------|-------------|
| Craft | No preservatives |
| Handmade | Organic |
| Homemade | Small batch |
| Traditional | Classic |

## State label regulations vs federal

The product label description for many products intended to be sold at a farmer's market will have better success if they focus on the handmade aspect of manufacturing. This is a big consumer draw for those seeking products at farmer's markets.

The consistency will also decide the product name. A thick sauce or paste would be labeled with the word "paste" and not necessarily "hot sauce"., although it is recommended to include the words "pepper", "hot" or "spicey" in the name of the product if it is descriptive of the sauce. The more information you can give to a consumer on a package label the better.

## Size of the bottle

Many specialty and sample hot sauces are packaged in 5 oz bottles. This may not give much surface to display the information required. Take this into consideration when designing the Product Display Panel for your hot sauce. The information on the PDP will be on the front-facing surface so this will give even less of an area to display information.

Graphics can be a huge part of marketing a new hot sauce product by using amusing artwork and colorful graphics. These can attract attention but also interfere with the label contents or become overbearing against the product name.

### Product Display Panel

Typically, a Product Display Panel (PDP) is on the face of the product that is front-facing and seen by the consumer. The Product Display Panel should be the most prominent display seen by the consumer and this is where specific requirements such as the name of the product and quantity or weight will be displayed.

Considering that a hot sauce bottle is round the front-facing surface would be where the PDP is placed. A portion of this will wrap around the bottle but the name of the product should be front-facing and visible. For a hot sauce, the PDP is often part of the other nutritional data and informational panel.

## Name of product

The name of the product or statement of identity should stand out on the PDP, but this does not include the brand name or logo. Marketing tactics have forced manufacturers to highlight the brand name on the bottle and make it bigger than the statement of identity, but the name of the product needs to be visible.

The FDA or statewide sanctioned farmer's markets do not regulate what you call the product, but a start-up brand of sauce should have the words "hot sauce" somewhere on the PDP. This statement could be embellished or changed to include the words gourmet, Louisiana style, or other words describing the product such as artisan, Caribbean, or craft.

## Information panel

The information panel will typically include the name and address of the manufacturer, packaging, or distributor and the nutritional information, ingredient list, and any allergy labeling. The information panel will be directly to the right of the PDP. Although products intended to be sold in retail business should have a bar code the FDA does not require that a hot sauce have one and neither do the cottage food laws in most states.

Additional information on the information panel will be allergen information and voluntary ingredients like vitamin contents if applicable. This side panel does not typically contain any artwork although there may be a minimized logo. This is not an FDA recommendation, but many manufacturers will include it toward the bottom right or left corner.

**Type (font) size**

The type or font size should be large, easy to read, and contrast with the background label. Although there is no FDA regulation with the length of the product description, "Tom's super-hot deluxe road burning tongue scorching hot sauce" may be difficult to display on such a small package. **Most label requirements per state cottage food laws require a specific font size.**

**Artwork**

Hot sauce labels and brand names are becoming more extravagant as unique ingredients and flavors are being introduced into hot sauce recipes. The artwork should not misrepresent the hot sauce. I do not see how a gentleman with his pants down, sitting on a toilet with flames coming out his rear is in any way a misrepresentation of the sauce. The FDA does not regulate hot sauce bottle designs which is why the names and artwork are often very extravagant. Local cottage food laws may or may not have specific requirements pertaining to graphics.

**Ingredients**

The ingredients should be listed in order by weight, and this is typically a labeling requirement per FDA sanctioned package labels. This also includes sub-ingredients, ingredients that are part of another product. There are specific requirements for what ingredients need to be included as part of your hot sauce recipe.

A percentage of the ingredients does not need to be declared on the label. There are specific requirements for juices, which are often part of gourmet hot sauces, but not necessary to be excluded as a percentage.

**Product quantity**

The net weight needs to be printed clearly on the packaging displaying the US customary and the metric measurement. This is a requirement in most states and is also a good common practice for consumer information. This would include the net weight of the hot sauce and not the packaging associated with it. The weight is also considered part of the label statement and should appear on the PDP, usually toward the bottom of the label.

The net quantity of contents or weight of the product should include all of the ingredients that constitute the end product of hot sauce, but the weight of each ingredient does not need to be listed. However, you should have this information documented somewhere for the purpose of making the sauce in large quantities.

**Food allergen**

The list of food allergens from the FDA covers about 90% of food allergies and fortunately many are not used in hot sauce recipes. If your hot sauce contains one of the items on the food allergen list thoroughly read section F1 – F16, then it needs to be included on the information panel. It is good practice to label a hot sauce as gluten-free, vegan, zero calories, or allergen-free…if it is. This is most likely a requirement per your states cottage food law to include an allergen statement.

## Common food allergens

| Soybean | Eggs | Sesame |
|---------|------|--------|
| Milk | Fish | Tree Nuts |
| Shellfish | Peanuts | Wheat |

### Nutritional label

There is not any specific information needed on the nutritional label including the order, even though your hot sauce may not include any of the information, it needs to be displayed. Only nutrients that are listed as mandatory or voluntary need to be included. Your hot sauce can be tested for nutritional value at a laboratory.

### Label size

There is not a limit to how big or how small a product label can be but generally speaking, the PDP, information panel, and bar code will be one label wrapped around a bottle of hot sauce. The FDA does not have any objections to this, but a 5 oz bottle will not provide much room to display product information.

### Where DON'T I need a label?

There are occasions where you do not need a product label on a hot sauce. If you plan on selling outside of retail stores or online shops, then a product label isn't needed.

Farmer's markets, craft fairs, or your restaurant may also not require labels to the extent that the FDA requires but it is a good communication practice. However, most of them do and will also have specific required statements.

What is great about hot sauce is that a woozy bottle makes it instantly recognizable as a hot sauce. If you own an establishment that provides food that pairs well with hot sauce then providing your hot sauce without a label would be fine.

### Reasons not to label a hot sauce

The reason NOT to label a hot sauce aside from the reason listed above is that it could be time-consuming and add additional costs.

If you have a new product, you are sampling then you may not want to put in the effort to design a label, purchase a nutritional label and a bar code until it has been widely accepted.

### Label companies

Many companies that provide labeling for hot sauce bottles will also provide design services. Hiring a professional to design your hot sauce graphics is important, even selling at a farm market, because the label can be a strong marketing focus.

Many times, the consumer has only the content on a label to help them decide to make a purchase or not.

## Labeling machines

Like a lot of pieces of equipment, there can be varying differences in products to include pricing, automated, manual, and the number of units produced per minute.

A start-up hot sauce company would probably want to use inexpensive manually operated machines. Labels can be applied to individual bottles by hand, but this increased the possibility that the labels could be off-set.

# Section 4

# Sell the Sauce

*Selling hot sauce at a farm market will be one of the few occasions where you are face to face with the customer and presented with an opportunity to make a sale*

## Selling

Simply having a hot sauce product packaged for sale with a professional-looking label may not always guarantee a sale. Much of your efforts at a farmer's market will focus on "making a sale" or verbally providing a sales pitch to a potential customer. The great thing about selling hot sauce at a farmer's market is that there will be plenty of one-on-one opportunities or customer interactions that will lead to the sales of your sauce.

## Sales pitch

Having a sales pitch or a pre-established statement to say to people that leads to sales will be necessary, but it will also benefit to have a good approachable demeaner. **Selling hot sauce at a farm market will be one of the few occasions where you are face to face with the customer and presented with an opportunity to make a sale.** This is where a prewritten and well thought out sales pitch will work towards making sales.

Decide how you want to market your product BEFORE you begin a sales campaign or set up at a farmer's market. This will direct your approach.

## 4 Marketing approaches for farm markets

### 1. You will be present

Farmer's markets are not intended to be automated and will usually require people presenting, sampling, and showcasing their products. You, or someone from your company will be present at the time of the sales. This can be a rare opportunity in the sales world.

### 2. Provide samples

Being present for customer interaction and providing samples can increase sales. Be prepared to offer suggestions on how to pair your hot sauce with food as well. If a customer knows how they are going to use your product when they walk away it means they have a better chance to consume it as intended. Hot sauce food pairing is extremely important.

### 3. Use promotional material

Promotional materials can help make a customer or potential customer walk away as though they have received something extra. If you can create them inexpensively and they can help promote your hot sauce after the purchase has been made.

### a. Recipe cards

Recipe cards that highlight your hot sauce with

73

an easy to make recipe like dips or sides. Most customers will consider you (the person making the sale) as the expert so the suggestions you make or recipes cards you hand out should bring them back purchasing more sauce.

### b. Giveaways

Pens, stickers, t-shirts, or anything with your logo are excellent giveaways but could be a costly marketing venture. They are like recipe cards but should have something particular to do with your sauce.

### c. Print materials

Print materials are relatively inexpensive to produce and can provide a customer with your URL, company name, logo, facts about your sauce, or other materials you provide to increase sales.

### 4. Consider your added value

Being yourself and standing behind your product can provide support for how your product stands up against the competitor.

### Licensing requirements

There are a few states that do not have any licensing requirements for selling hot sauce at a farm market. Although the requirements could be slightly different per each jurisdiction the process of filing a form along with a payment will be similar.

**There are 24 States that allow hot sauce to be sold as a cottage food.** In many states, if hot sauce is not approved as a cottage food spices, dried pepper, hot jellies or honey are.

| States allowing hot sauce sold under cottage laws | | |
|---|---|---|
| Alabama | Minnesota | Pennsylvania |
| Alaska | Mississippi | Rhode Island |
| Arkansas | Montana | South Dakota |
| Illinois | Nevada | Texas |
| Iowa | North Carolina | Utah |
| Louisiana | North Dakota | Virginia |
| Maine | Oklahoma | Wisconsin |
| Maryland | Oregon | Wyoming |

## States with exceptions to cottage food laws

Many states that do not allow the sale of homemade hot sauce or other products through local cottage food laws will have exemptions.

## Reading this table

I condensed the requirements needed to sell homemade hot in each state into 5 easy to read tables. Although requirements and always changing it takes a while to make a drastic jump for not accepting hot sauce as a cottage food to allowing it for sale at a farmer's market.

## Approved

"Approved" means that a hot sauce product is approved for sale directly to consumers without going through FDA regulations.

## FDA Guidelines

FDA guidelines can be followed at local farm markets, but it is not necessary in many states. Even if you hot sauce follows FDA regulations its possible it will not get accepted at local farmer's markets, with or without proper pH test results.

## Sales cap

Many states will limit the amount of sales that

can be made annually from homemade hot sauce. However, this can also make a great opportunity for entrepreneurship. Limiting sales projections can also help create a budget and hinder overspending.

**Permits**

This can be a very broad category because most farm markets will require to have at least a temporary permit to set up and sell hot sauce. This is usually easy to obtain through the local agricultural department or organization running the farm market. Costs vary between farmer's market, but they are generally not more than a few hundred dollars.

**pH testing**

Many states will require laboratory-documented pH testing but others may not require any at all. This is to ensure that your hot sauce is below a pH of 4.6 or has enough acidity to be "safe" for consumers.

**Online sales**

Very few states allow homemade hot sauce to be sold online through their cottage food laws and many that do allow pick up only.

| State | Approved | FDA Guidelines | Sales cap | Permits | pH testing | Online sales |
|---|---|---|---|---|---|---|
| Alabama | Yes | No | No | Yes | No | Yes |
| Alaska | Yes | No | Yes | No | Yes | Yes |
| Arizona | No | Yes | No | No | Yes | Yes |
| Arkansas | Yes | No | No | No | No | Yes |
| California | No | Yes | No | No | Yes | Yes |
| Colorado | No | Yes | No | No | Yes | Yes |
| Connecticut | No | Yes | No | No | Yes | Yes |
| Delaware | No | Yes | No | No | Yes | Yes |
| Florida | No | Yes | No | No | Yes | Yes |
| Georgia | No | Yes | No | No | Yes | Yes |

| State | Approved | FDA Guidelines | Sales cap | Permits | pH testing | Online sales |
|-------|----------|----------------|-----------|---------|------------|--------------|
| Hawaii | No | Yes | No | Yes | Yes | Yes |
| Idaho | No | Yes | No | Yes | Yes | Yes |
| Illinois | Yes | No | No | Yes | Yes | No |
| Indiana | No | Yes | No | Yes | Yes | Yes |
| Iowa | Yes | No | No | No | No | Yes |
| Kansas | No | Yes | No | Yes | Yes | Yes |
| Kentucky | Yes | No | Yes | Yes | Yes | No |
| Louisiana | Yes | No | Yes | No | No | Yes |
| Maine | Yes | No | No | Yes | Yes | Yes |
| Maryland | Yes | No | Yes | Yes | Yes | No |

| State | Approved | FDA Guidelines | Sales cap | Permits | pH testing | Online sales |
|---|---|---|---|---|---|---|
| Massachusetts | No | Yes | No | No | Yes | Yes |
| Michigan | No | Yes | No | Yes | Yes | Yes |
| Minnesota | Yes | No | Yes | Yes | No | Yes |
| Mississippi | Yes | No | Yes | No | No | No |
| Missouri | No | Yes | No | No | Yes | Yes |
| Montana | Yes | No | No | No | No | Yes |
| Nebraska | No | Yes | No | Yes | Yes | Yes |
| Nevada | Yes | No | Yes | Yes | Yes | Yes |
| New Hampshire | No | Yes | No | No | Yes | Yes |
| New Jersey | No | Yes | No | No | Yes | Yes |

| State | Approved | FDA Guidelines | Sales cap | Permits | pH testing | Online sales |
|---|---|---|---|---|---|---|
| New Mexico | No | Yes | No | Yes | Yes | Yes |
| New York | No | Yes | No | Yes | Yes | Yes |
| North Caro | Yes | No | No | Yes | Yes | Yes |
| North Dakota | Yes | No | No | No | No | No |
| Ohio | No | Yes | No | Yes | Yes | Yes |
| Oklahoma | Yes | No | Yes | No | No | Yes |
| Oregon | Yes | No | No | Yes | Yes | Yes |
| Pennsylvania | Yes | No | No | Yes | Yes | Yes |
| Rhode Island | Yes | N | No | Yes | Yes | No |
| South Carolina | No | Yes | No | No | Yes | Yes |

| State | Approved | FDA Guidelines | Sales cap | Permits needed | pH testing | Online sales |
|---|---|---|---|---|---|---|
| South Dakota | Yes | No | No | No | No | Yes |
| Tennessee | Yes | Yes | No | No | No | Yes |
| Texas | Yes | No | Yes | No | Yes | Yes |
| Utah | No | Yes | No | Yes | Yes | Yes |
| Vermont | Yes | No | Yes | No | No | Yes |
| Virginia | Yes | No | Yes | No | No | No |
| Washington | No | Yes | Yes | No | Yes | Yes |
| West Virginia | No | Yes | No | No | Yes | Yes |
| Wisconsin | Yes | No | Yes | No | Yes | No |
| Wyoming | Yes | No | Yes | No | No | Yes |

## Sales cap for states approving hot sauce as a cottage food

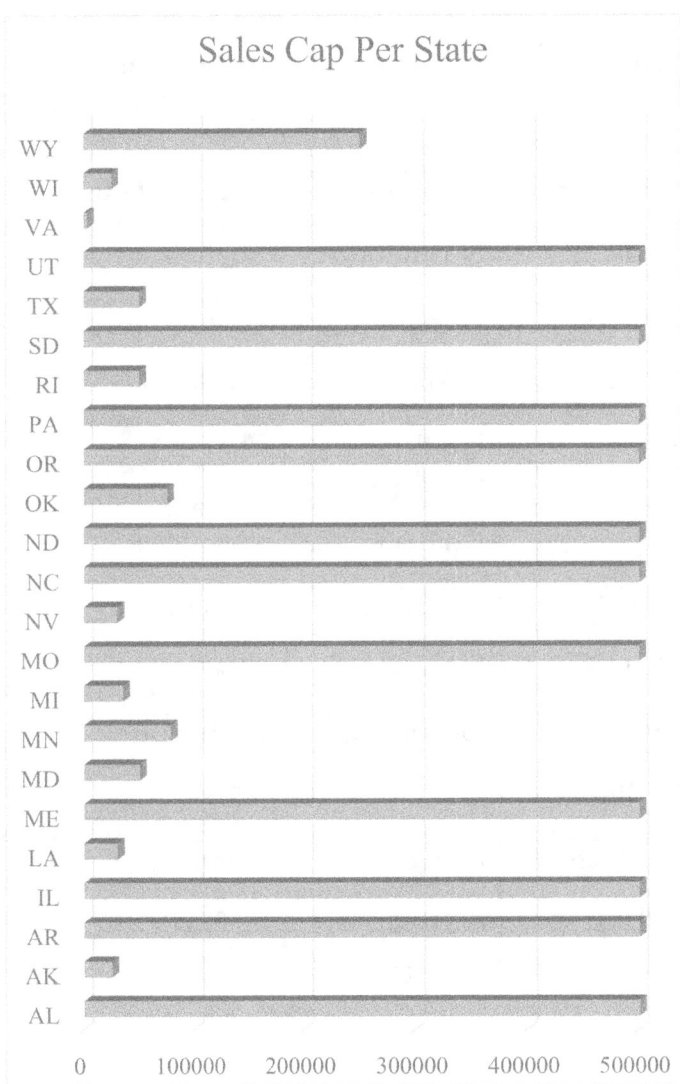

| Alabama | Minnesota | Pennsylvania |
|---|---|---|
| No limit | $78,000 | No limit |
| Alaska | Mississippi | Rhode Island |
| $25,000 | $35,000 | $50,000 |
| Arkansas | Montana | South Dakota |
| No limit | No limit | No limit |
| Illinois | Nevada | Texas |
| No limit | $35,000 | $50,000 |
| Iowa | North Carolina | Utah |
| No limit | No limit | No limit |
| Louisiana | North Dakota | Virginia |
| $30,000 | No limit | $3,000 |
| Maine | Oklahoma | Wisconsin |
| No limit | $75,000 | $25,000 |
| Maryland | Oregon | Wyoming |
| $50,000 | No limit | $250,000 |

# Alabama

**Alabama Public Health Department**
**(334) 240 7247**
**(877) 774 9519**
**fma@agi.alabama.gov**

Under the Cottage Food Law (Alabama Senate Bill 160) hot sauce cannot be processed in a home kitchen and sold at markets, therefore FDA regulations will need to be followed. This means that commercial kitchen space will need to be licensed with the FDA even though you intend to sell at local farm market.

Alabama is one of the few states with a "gray" area of allowed foods under their cottage food laws where hot sauce is not clearly stated as being approved. If you are making an acidified sauce, you are probably ok, but you may be safer if you follow FDA guidelines. Contact the Alabama Public Health Department or Farmer's Market Authority directly for more information on selling hot sauce at a farmer's market. State regulations in Alabama are very stringent but following federal FDA guidelines for manufacturing a hot sauce will provide the state with the necessary to sell at a farm market.

# Alaska

**Cooperative Extension**
**(907) 474 5211**
**cesweb@alaska.edu**

**Alaska State Environmental Health Laboratory**
**(907) 375 8231**
**dec.eh-lab-shippingreceiving@alaska.gov**

Many states allow acidified foods like hot sauce to be manufactured but they will need proof that the hot sauce "non-potentially hazardous food". In the state of Alaska, although hot sauce is not listed as an approved food, if it has a pH below 4.6 it could get approved under the cottage food laws because a product with a pH below 4.6 are acidified enough to kill harmful bacteria and make a hot sauce nonhazardous. Although there is a $25,000 sales cap limiting how much homemade hot sauce can be sold to consumers the state of Alaska allows sales anywhere without restrictions. However, you will need to provide lab results that your hot sauce has a pH below 4.6. Cottage food laws in the state of Alaska vary slightly between jurisdictions.

# Arizona

**Arizona Department of Health Services**
**www.azdhs.gov**
**(602) 364 3120**
**cottagefood@azdhs.gov**

**Arizona Department of Agriculture**
**(602) 543 4373**

Arizona does not have a cottage food law that allows the sale of homemade hot sauce from a home kitchen, at a farm market or otherwise. Starting a hot sauce business with the intention to sell at a farm market will require following FDA regulations. If your hot sauce has a pH at or below 4.6, contact the Arizona Cottage Food Program to see if you qualify. You'll also need to take their food handler training.

Many states are continually amending their cottage food programs to accept different foods such as hot sauce to support startup business. However, items such as hot honey, dry spices, or spicy jellies can get approved for sale. Another benefit to this cottage food law is that there isn't a sales cap so there is the potential to make a decent amount of money.

# Arkansas

## Arkansas Department of Public Health
## (501) 661 2678

## Arkansas Farmer's Market Association
## (501) 712-2002
## Katrina.betancourt@arkansasobesity.org

Arkansas has one of the best cottage food programs for making and selling hot sauce out of your home for the purpose of selling it at a farm market. However, like many states that approve hot sauce under the cottage food laws, the bottles will need to be labeled with specific requirements stating that the hot sauce was made in a facility that has not been inspected.

A homemade hot sauce sold in Arkansas may need to be acidified to a pH below 4.6 but there is no sales cap. A permit may be required specifically for the sale of hot sauce.

# California

**California Department of Public Health Food &
Drug Branch**
**(916) 650 6500**
**(800) 495 3232**
**www.fdbretail@cdph.ca.gov**

**Certified Farmers' Markets**
**(916) 900 5030**
**cfm@cdfa.ca.gov**

California has 844 farm markets throughout the
state. Under the MHKO act food can be sold to
customers on the same day it is made but this
does not include an acidified hot sauce. You may
be able to slide hot sauce under this law. Utah
has also adopted this. Unfortunately, it only
applies to some specific cities and counties
within the state of California.

However, cottage food operators can request to
have their hot sauce approved through the email
above on their provided form.

# Colorado

**Department of Public Health & Environment**
**(303) 692 3645**
**www.cdphe_mfgfd@state.co.us**

**Colorado Farmer's Market Coalition**
**www.cofarmersmarkets.org**

Selling hot sauce at a farmer's market in the state of Colorado requires following FDA guidelines. Colorado has an OK cottage food law, but it does not allow the manufacture and sale of hot sauce out of a home established kitchen. Call the Department of Public Health & Environment for the most current information.

Many of these food laws are amended all the time to accommodate trend in food consumption like hot sauces or try selling other foods like spicy pickled vegetables. Colorado is another state that has a "grey" area that does not clearly define the approval of hot sauces. Generally speaking, your hot sauce has a better chance of being approved if you can provide laboratory testing results indicating it is "non-potentially hazardous".

# Connecticut

**Connecticut Department of Consumer Protection, Food and Standards Division**
**(860) 713-6160**
**dcp.foodandstandards@ct.gov**

**Connecticut Farm Fresh Cooperative Association**
**info@ctfarmfresh.org**

Connecticut does not allow the sale of homemade hot sauce directly to consumers through a farm market or otherwise. All manufacturing and sales will need to follow FDA regulations like many other states.

The states cottage food guidelines are nearly as stringent as federal requirements so once approved by the FDA you will simply need to locate farm markets and apply for their permits.

However, spicy products can come in many different forms such as jams, jellies, and dried spices. The kitchen area where you prepare these foods will still require a local jurisdiction to inspect and pass.

# Delaware

**Delaware Department of Health & Social Services**
**Office of Food Protection – Cottage Food Establishment**
**(302) 744 4700**

Unfortunately, Delaware is known to have one of the worst cottage food laws working against the sale of homemade hot sauce directly to consumers.

However, farmers to have a wider range of products allowed for sale under the Delaware cottage food laws. Some of these items include spicy herbs, syrups, and honey.

The state of Delaware requires that the hot sauce intended to be sold at a farmer's be registered through the FDA.

However, you will also have to go through a process of approval through the local operators of the farm market you choose.

# Florida

**Florida Department of Agriculture and Consumer Services**
**(850) 245 5520**
**FoodSafety@FDACS.gov**

**Florida Farmer's Market Association**
**(352) 377 6345**

Many states allow acidified foods like hot sauce to be manufactured and sold without following federal regulations, but the state of Florida is not one of them. If you reside in Florida and want to sell hot sauce at a farm market, follow the Federal Food and Drug Administration guidelines for hot sauce production.

The idea behind cottage food laws is support food products that are grown and produced locally. If your hot sauce is produced locally and following FDA regulations some farm markets in the state of Florida may accept it. Otherwise, dried spices, hot honey can be sold under a very high salary cap of $250,000.

# Georgia

**Georgia Department of Agriculture**
**Retail Food Program**
**(404) 656 3627**
**retailfoodinfo@arg.georgia.gov**

**Cottage Food Program**
**CottageFoodInfo@agr.georgia.gov**
**(404) 656-3627**
**(855) 424-5423**
**gdalicensing@agr.georgia.gov**

The state of Georgia does not allow the sale of homemade hot sauce at farmer's markets and setting up sales for other cottage foods like dried spices can also be very difficult as well.

Hot sauce manufacturing and sales will follow FDA regulations, but the permit process will follow the local farm market organization of your choice. Because cottage food laws are changing constantly to include and accept different types of foods including hot sauces selling at a farm market doesn't stop there. Once approved by the FDA you can sell your hot sauce anywhere with the proper permit.

# Hawaii

**Hawaii Department of Agriculture**
**(808) 973-9560**
**hdoa.info@hawaii.gov**

**Hawaii Farmers market association**
**www.harmonee@sustainablemolokai.org**

**Hawaii Farm Bureau**
**(808) 848 2074**
**info@hfbf.org**

Hawaii is another state that does not have the best laws for homemade hot sauce that is produced for the purpose of selling at a farmer's market. Fermented hot sauce or a hot sauce with pH below 4.6 like many other states is not approved for sale through the local cottage food laws. Once your hot sauce has been produced in an FDA approved state you may be able to sell it at other festivals and events. This makes a great opportunity to begin a hot sauce business with unlimited income because the cottage food laws in Hawaii to not have sales caps. Other options include selling stores or online retailers.

# Idaho

**Idaho Department of Health & Welfare**
**(208) 334 5938**
**foodprotection@dhw.idaho.gov**

**Idaho Farmers Market Association**
**(208) 614 2292**
**info@idahofma.org**
**www.idahofma.org**

**Idaho Food Cottage Program**
**(208) 334 5938**
**foodprotection@dhw.idaho.gov**

Idaho does not allow the sale of homemade hot sauce as an acidified food under any of their local cottage food laws. Therefore, all processing, production, manufacturing, bottling, and labeling will need to be done at a manufacturing facility registered through the FDA.

Once you have followed these guidelines, you can sell at any farm market in the US if the local jurisdiction within that state has approved your hot sauce.

# Illinois

**Illinois Department of Public Health**
**(217) 782 4977**
**(312) 814 2793**
**(312) 814 5278**

**Illinois Department of Agriculture**
**Springfield Office - Administrative**
**Headquarters**
**(217) 782 2172**

**Illinois Farmers Market Association**
**www.ilfma.org**

You do not need to follow FDA guidelines to manufacture and sell hot sauce directly to consumers at a farm market in Illinois. Illinois has an excellent cottage food program for selling homemade hot sauce. Illinois allows the manufacture of hot sauce in a home kitchen and unlimited sales, unlike cottage food laws in many states. There is also the possibility of online sales or mail delivery although some types of hot sauces may not qualify. Be prepared to have your hot sauce laboratory tested with proven results.

# Indiana

**Indiana State Department of Health**
**(317) 234 8569**
**lharriso@isdh.in.gov**

**Indiana Farmer's Market**
**cferroli@icdp.coop**

**Farmer's Market Association**
**(317) 662 0354**
**info@hoosierfarmersmarkets.org**
**www.hoosierfarmersmarkets.org**

**F armer's Market Coalition**
**info@farmersmarketcoaliton.org**

Like many states Indiana does not approve the manufacturing and sale of hot sauce out of a home kitchen no matter what the pH level is. All registration and licensing requirements will follow FDA through local agricultural of health departments. Filing for permits to set up operations and sell hot sauce at a farmer's market will follow the local health authority conditions.

# Iowa

**Iowa Department of Inspections & Appeals**
**(515) 281 7102**
**tina.ahlberg@dia.iowa.gov**

**Iowa Farmer's Market Association**
**(319) 458 9396**

It can be easy to set up a hot sauce business in Iowa under the Iowa Cottage Food Law, making sauce out of your home and selling it at local farm markets directly to consumers.

As with many hot sauces that get approved through local cottage laws, your hot sauce needs to be acidified to a pH level at or below 4.6. This is to ensure that the product will not allow harmful bacterial growth. There will still need to be a process of getting it approved and accepted though local farm market associations.

The state of Iowa does not have a sales cap for selling hot sauce at a farmer's market but there will be a cost for setting up temporary operations.

# Kansas

**Kansas Dept of Agriculture Food Safety & Lodging**
**(785) 564 6767**
**kda.fsi@ks.gov**

**Cowley Farmer's Market Association**
**(620) 660 8953**
**cowleyfarmersmarketassociation@gmail.com**
**mercedes.taylorpuckett@gmail.com**

Kansas has a lot of *gray area* in their food sales when it comes to selling hot sauce at farmers markets. Hot sauce is not approved for sale as a cottage food but requires a Kansas Department of Agriculture Food Establishment License. The requirements for selling hot sauce in the state of Kansas are as stringent if you make a hot honey, pepper jelly or pepper vinegar. However, once approved there isn't a limit to the amount of sales your hot sauce can make and sales can be made online if sold within state limits. As of 2022 there were 95 farm markets available to sell homemade hot sauce providing that you can obtain the proper licensing. For many states like Kansas, acidified and non-acidified hot sauce will require the same type of licensing requirements.

# Kentucky

**Kentucky Department of Public Health, Food Safety Branch**
**502 564 7181**
**food.safety@ky.gov**

**Kentucky Farm Bureau**
**fran.mccall@kyfb.com**
**(502) 495 5000**

The state of Kentucky allows individuals to make and sell hot sauce from a home under the Kentucky Home-Based Microprocessor. Under this requirement the dominant ingredient must be grown by the producer of the hot sauce. This is to support the efforts of farms and self-produced products across the state.

Home based micro-processors must obtain the proper licensing and permits and must also attend a micro-processing workshop. In addition, the venues are limited to sales at their own farms, registered farm markets and certified roadside stands.

# Louisiana

**Louisiana Agriculture Department**
**(866) 927 2476**

**Louisiana Farm Bureau**
**(225) 922-6200**

Hot sauce is an approved cottage food in the state of Louisiana but has a sales cap of $30,000 annually under the cottage food law. Like many other states,

Louisiana has a sales cap that limits the amount of income you can earn from making and selling hot sauce out of your home and directly to consumers, but you can sell your hot sauce almost anywhere, to include online sales.

Louisiana is the birthplace of hot sauce Getting started is easier then some states because there isn't any testing, licensing, or inspections needed, only specific labelling requirements.

# Maine

**Department of Agriculture, Conservation & Forestry**
**(207) 287 3200**
**dacf@maine.gov**

**Maine Federation of Farmer's Markets**
**(207) 370-1524**

The state of Maine allows the sale of homemade hot sauce under their cottage food laws. Different types of foods are approved under Home Food Manufacturing law verses the Maine Food Sovereignty Law. Licensing as a Home Food Manufacture requires additional application procedures but allows less restrictions for sales.

Sales under the Maine Home Food Manufacturing law allows for online orders and mail delivery Sales can also be made on hot sauces and dried spices at local markets without an annual sales cap. The only exception of the Home Food Manufacturing law is the exemption from selling fermented foods, which some hot sauces can fall under.

# Maryland

**Department of Health**
**(410) 767 8400**

**Department of Agriculture**
**(410) 841-5769**

Maryland has a Cottage Food Law and a On-Farm Home Processing licence but only the latter allows for the sale of homemade hot sauce. **However,** the state of Maryland does allow the sale of dried spices with a $50,000 sales cap. Apply for an On Farm Processing License to expand into the sales of hot sauces.

Do I need to be a farmer to sell hot sauce on a farm? Contact Maryland Agriculture Resource Based Industry Development Corporation (MARBIDCO ) at (410) 267 6807 for what qualifies as a farm. Once establishing a license, either through the Maryland Cottage Food Law or On Farm Processing license sales can be made online and delivered directly to consumers.

# Massachusetts

**Massachusetts Department of Public Health
Food Protection Program
(617) 983 6712
fpp.dph@state.ma.us**

**Mass Farmer's Market
781-893-8222
hello@massfarmersmarkets.org**

Massachusetts does not allow the sale of homemade hot sauce under their cottage food laws. Manufacturing hot sauce in a home kitchen and selling it at a farm market will require following FDA regulations.

**However,** both spicy jellies and dried spices are allowed. For Massachusetts and many **states,** it is the way the product is processed. With over 350 farm markets, Massachusetts offers up a lot of opportunities to start a hot sauce or dried **spice business**. Once approved under the Massachusetts cottage food law there isn't any sales cap on the amount of revenue that can be earned.

# Michigan

**Michigan Department of Agriculture and Rural Development**
**(800) 292 3939**

**Michigan Farmer's Market Association**
**(517) 432-3381**

Michigan does not allow the manufacture and sale from a home kitchen under their cottage law, therefore all operations will need to follow FDA regulations.

However spicy jellies and spices are classified are foods that do not require time and temperature control and are therefore acceptable.

However, there is a $25,000 sales cap and online sales are not allowed regardless of the product.

# Minnesota

**Minnesota Department of Agriculture**
**(651) 201 6027**
**mda.foodlicensingliason@state.mn.us**

**Minnesota Farmer's Market Association**
**(507) 664-9446**

Minnesota is an average state to sell homemade hot sauce under their cottage food laws. Like many states, the sauce needs to be a pH of 4.6 or lower, labeling needs to have specific statements, and you will need to take a food preparer training course.

Another way to look at this would be potentially hazardous shelf stable foods or foods that do not require refrigeration. Therefore, both hot sauces and spices would qualify as a cottage food but with an annual sales cap of $78,000. Additional fees for a food safety training course also apply.

# Mississippi

**Mississippi Department of Health**
**(866) 458 4948**
**(601) 576 7400**

**Mississippi Farmer's Markets**
**farmersmarket@mdac.ms.gov**
**(601) 354 6573**

Hot sauce is approved under Mississippi's cottage food law if the pH is at 4.6 or below. However, there is a sales limit to how much annual **sales you** can have and restriction for how it is sold as well.

Selling dried peppers, hot jelly or spicy pickles are also allowed but will fall under the same $35,000 sales cap. However, no online sale or mail delivery through Mississippi's cottage food law. Sales directly to restaurants and stores are not allowed.

# Missouri

**Missouri Department of Health**
**(573) 751 6095**
**info@health.mo.gov**

**Missouri Farmer's Market Association**
**www.missourifarmersmarkets.org**

The state of Missouri has very stringent requirements when it comes to selling hot sauce though their cottage laws. In Missouri the type of hot sauce doesn't make much of a difference because cottage food is decided by the establishment where it is made.

However, selling dried spices is acceptable as well as spicy jellies. Once approved there is no sales cap but mail deliveries, online orders or not, are not allowed.

# Montana

**Montana Department of Public Health & Human Services**
**(800) 362 8312**

**Montana Farmer's Market Network**
**farmersmarketmt.com**
**maurah@ncat.org**

Overall Montana is a great state for making and selling homemade hot sauces or dried spices. Making and selling hot sauce in a home kitchen was illegal in Montana up until 2015 but it now fall under the 2021 Local Food Choice Act as being an acceptable homemade product to sell directly to consumers. This includes online sales and mail delivery.

A separate permit is needed for a Temporary Food Establishment if you are selling at farmer's markets, fairs, or community events.

Compared to other states, Montana does not have as many farm market options as others states with.

# Nebraska

**Nebraska Department of Agriculture, Food Safety & Consumer Protection**
**(402) 471 3422**
**agr.webmaster@nebraska.gov**

**Nebraska Farmer's Market Association**
**www.nefarmersmarkets.org**
**www.buylocalnebraska.org**

Hot sauce manufacturing though a home kitchen and sales and sales directly to consumers are not allowed through the cottage food law of Nebraska, called the Pure Food Act. All manufacturing and sales of hot sauce will follow FDA regulations like many hot sauces do on the commercial level. However, dried pepper powder can be made in a home kitchen and sold directly to consumers through online retailers, farm markets, or other venues with no restrictions to annual sales.

There are over 100 farm markets across the state. Although these is a licensing and food handler training requirements, there are not any inspections or lab testing requirements.

# Nevada

**Nevada Department of Public health**
**Division of Agriculture**
**(775) 353 3600**

**Nevada Grown**
**(775) 351 2551**
**louhela.ann@gmail.com**
**www.nevadagrown.com**
**info@knowwhereyourfoodcomesfrom.com**

Hot sauce can be manufactured as a cottage food under in a home kitchen and sold directly to consumers through the craft food registration if the sauce is 4.6 pH or below. Don't assume that your hot sauce is below a safe pH level and test it frequently to determine if it fluctuates. However, there is a sales cap of $35,000 and Nevada restricts online sales. There are no restrictions where hot sauce can be sold as long as it is face to face.

For the size of the state, Nevada does not have as many farm market opportunities to sell hot sauce and spices as some other states do.

# New Hampshire

**New Hampshire Department of Health and Human Services**
**(603) 271 4589**
**DHHS.foodprotection@dhhs.nh.gov**

**New Hampshire Farm Bureau Federation**
**(603) 224-1934**

New Hampshire does not allow the sale of homemade hot sauce to consumers, acidified or not. New Hampshire has a decent cottage food law regardless of hot sauce being allowed under the New Hampshire Exempt Home Food Operation, but the New Hampshire Homestead law may have different requirements. No food handler training, or inspection of facilities is needed but a permit is required under the New Hampshire Homestead law. Spices, pepper powders and dried hot peppers can be sold directly to consumers.

Contact the New Hampshire Department of Health and Human Services for more information or the New Hampshire Department of Agriculture, Markets & Food for a list of farmers markets.

# New Jersey

**New Jersey Department of Health**
**(609) 913 5099**
**cfo@doh.nj.gov**

**New Jersey Council of Farmers and**
**Communities**
**Jackie.Bavaro@yalliance.org**

**New Jersey's Farmer's, Markets & Growers**
**Coalition**
**www.jersyfarmersmarket.com**
**(607) 393 4763**

Unfortunately, New Jersey does not have a cottage food law that allows homemade hot sauce to be sold directly to consumers. It's not the spiciness or acidity that is the issue but how it is made and preserved. However, a dried spice business can be an easy and successful endeavor under New Jersey cottage food laws. Depending on the spice combination you may need to file an application with the New Jersy Public Health and Food Protection Program. New Jersey has a sales cap of $50,000 annually and there is a food handler training program that needs to be completed.

# New Mexico

**Environmental Health Bureau Food Program Manager (505) 222 9515**
**www.mewmexicofma.org**

**New Mexico Farmer's Market Association**
**www.farmersmarketsnm.org**

The state of New Mexico does not approve the manufacture and sale of hot sauce out of a home kitchen. All production, registration, permits, licensing, and sales of hot sauce at a farmer's Market need to follow FDA regulations. Although there is not a specific list, approved foods are limited to Non-TCS (Non-Temperature Control for Food Safety), making dehydrated peppers, dried **spices,** or spicy jams acceptable.

What makes New Mexico a great state to sell spicy foods is that there is no sales cap, no food handler training, and no food testing needed. Contact the New Mexico Farmers Market Association for more information sell spicy food at a local farmers market.

# New York

**New York State Department of Agriculture and Markets**
**ceheduc@health.ny.gov**
**(800) 554 4501**

**Farmer's Market Federation of New York**
**(315) 400-1447**

To manufacture hot sauce in New York State you need a 20-C Food Processing License because hot sauce is not allowed to be processed under a home processing exemption like many other foods are. Local cottage food laws do not approve hot sauce as a shelf stable product that can be manufactured in a home kitchen and sold directly to consumers, no matter what the pH level is.

However, spicy jams, jellies and dried spices or other types of spicy snacks are accepted. Startup for a spicy food business that focuses on foods approved under the local cottage food laws could be very lucrative with no annual sales cap, no inspections and no further food handler training.

# North Carolina

**North Carolina Department of Agriculture and Consumer Services, Food and Drug Protection Division**
**reagan.converse@ncagr.gov**
**(919) 733 7366**

**Farmer's Market Association of North Carolina**
**(910) 840-6743**

North Carolina allows the sale of homemade hot sauce directly to consumers if the sauce is laboratory approved to have a pH below 4.6. The documentation from a credible laboratory will need to be submitted to the local cottage food authority representative. Test your hot sauce at home frequently before you consider sending it to a laboratory.

This will save a lot of unnecessary steps to submit it several times. North Carolina has no limit to annual sales either directly to consumers or through online sales.

# North Dakota

**North Dakota Health and Human Services**
dhseo@nd.gov
(701) 328 2316

**North Dakata Farmer's Market and Growers Association**
ndfmga@outlook.com
(701) 871 7304

North Dakota Cottage Food Law states that *"as long as the food does not require refrigeration or contain meat"* it can be sold as cottage food, so that covers many types of hot sauces.

Like many states, the labeling requires that it must specifically state that it is *"produced in a home kitchen, without inspection. This product is made in a home kitchen that is not inspected by state or local health department"*. North Dakota has no limit to annual sales, but all sales need to be made directly to consumers and not online.

# Ohio

**Ohio Department of Agriculture**
**(617) 728 6250**
**foodsafety@agri.ohio.gov**

**Ohio Farm Bureau**
**www.ofbf.org**

Acidified foods such as a low pH hot sauce is not allowed to be sold under the cottage food law of Ohio. All manufacturing and sales will need to follow FDA regulations.

 If you are making and selling spicy jams, jellies and honeys under the Ohio cottage food law things look good with no sales limit, and no inspections or special licensing.

After your hot sauce gets approved through the FDA there are over 400 farm markets in the state of Ohio to sell it.

# Oklahoma

**Oklahoma Consumer Health Service**
**consumerHealth@health.ok.gov**

**Oklahoma Department of Agriculture, Food & Forestry Agritourism Program**

**(405) 522 5560**

Your chances of getting your hot sauce approved for sale at local farm markets in Oklahoma are good. Cottage food sales in Oklahoma are classified by those that need time or temperature control and those that do not. Any hot sauce containing seafood, poultry and meat is not approved but fortunately not many hot sauces contain these ingredients. Oklahoma has a sales cap of $75,000 annually but online sales are allowed.

There are very few homemade products that are not allowed for sales under the Oklahoma Food Freedom Act.

# Oregon

**Food Safety**
**(503) 986 4720**

**Oregon Farmer's Market Association**
**(503) 217 4010**

Selling hot sauce in the state of Oregon is allowed under the Oregon Farm Direct program and the Oregon Domestic Kitchen license.

Spicy foods, hot honey and dried spices will also prosper because the state of Oregon has over 190 farm markets.

There is no sales cap under the Oregon Domestic Kitchen law, but a home kitchen will need an inspection. Laboratory testing will be needed to determine if your hot sauce is acidified.

# Pennsylvania

**Pennsylvania Department of Agriculture**
ra-foodsafety@pa.gov
rhein@pa.gov
(717) 787-5107
(223) 666-2568

**Farmer's Market Coalition**
bfm3@psu.edu
(610) 391 9840

Pennsylvania allows the sale of hot sauce directly to consumers at farm markets or online through their cottage food laws. This also includes the sale of spicy salsa, fermented hot sauces or other shelf stable sauces. There is also no sales cap and no food safety training requirement, making this a great state to sell hot sauce at a farm market. Pennsylvania makes it easy to sell your homemade hot sauce directly to consumers just about anywhere to include restaurants, grocery stores, or online retailers.

In a addition, confirming your home kitchen as a Pennsylvania Limited Food Establishment allows your hot sauce or spicy food to be sold across state lines.

# Rhode Island

**Rhode Island Department of Health**
**Office of Food Protection**
**(401) 222 2749**

**Farm Fresh Rhode Island**
**www.farmfreshri.org**
**(401) 312 4250**

An acidified hot sauce can be sold directly to consumers in Rhode Island if it is manufactured in a kitchen on a farm. Rhode Island lists foods that are non-potentially hazardous and foods that do not need refrigeration.

Like other similar states the approval of hot sauce is not always clearly defined. Unfortunately, online sales are prohibited but getting started at a farm market is easy. Under the Rhode Island Non-Farmer Cottage Law hot sauce cannot be sold as this mostly covers the standard breads, cookies, and cakes.

# South Carolina

**South Carolina Department of Health & Environmental Control**
**info@dhec.sc.gov**
**(803) 898 3301**

**South Carolina Association of Farmers Markets**
**(803) 734 0328**

Many states allow acidified foods like hot sauce to be manufactured in a home kitchen and sold directly to consumers without following many regulations, but South Carolina is not one of them.

If you manufacture Spicy snacks like popcorn, sales can be made directly out of your home, at roadside stands, farm markets, grocery stores, restaurants, or online retailers.

In addition, your approved spicy food sales virtually need very little inspections, lessening, or training before sales can be made.

# South Dakota

**South Dakota Department of Health**
**(605) 773 4945**

**South Dakoata Farmer's Markets**
**(605) 681 6793**

**Farmer's Market Coalition**
**farmersmarketcoalition.org**

South Dakata has a pretty good cottage food law that allows the sale of homemade hot sauce directly to consumers. Producers of homemade hot sauce may produce "non-temperature controlled home processed canned goods" directly to consumers without a sales cap.

This law also includes spicy pickles, jellies, and many spicy homemade snacks. With almost nor restrictions on where your sauce can be sold, and no sales cap South Dakota comes out on top as being one of the better states to sell homemade hot sauce in. However, orders can be received online, but they cannot be shipped.

# Tennessee

**Tennessee Department of Agriculture**
**(615) 837 5193**

**Customer & Industry Services Food Safety**
**newfood.business@tn.gov**
**www.tn.gov/agriculture**
**(615) 837 5193**

**Tennessee association of Famer's Markets**
**info@tnfarmersmarkets.org**
**www.tnfarmersmarket.org**

Tennessee allows the manufacture and sale of shelf stable hot sauces out of a home kitchen under Tennessee Food Freedom Act 862. Unlike many other states, hot sauce can be sold wholesale to other stores within state lines as well.

Getting started is easy with very few licensing requirements, sauce testing or food handling requirements. Compared to many other states Tennessee is one of the better states to sell homemade hot sauce or spicy food in.

# Texas

**Texas Health and Human Services**
**(512) 776 7111**
**customer.service@dshs.texas.gov**

**Certified Farmer's Markets**
**(800) 835 5832**

**Texas Farmer's Market**
**www.texasfarmersmarket.org**
**Texas Network of Farmers Markets Resource**
**Center**
**askme@texaslocalfood.org**

Texas allows the manufacture and sale of homemade acidified foods like hot sauce, but the pH needs to be at or below 4.6 as many states also require. This means the sauce will need to be tested in a laboratory that provides results and these results will need to be presented to the cottage food authority in your jurisdiction.

The only downside is that the cottage food laws in Texas limit annual sales to $50,000, after that your business will need to follow federal regulations.

# Utah

**Department of Agriculture and Food**
**(801) 982-2200**

**Utah Agriculturally Affiliated Organizations**
**(801) 233 3006**

**Utah Farmer's Market Network**
**info@utahfarmersmarketnetwork.org**

Utah has three (3) different laws for making homemade hot sauce and spicy foods and selling them directly to consumers. Under the Cottage Food Act, hot sauce has no restrictions on sales or consumption.

The Homemade Food Act states food needs to be consumed at a residence and the Microenterprise Act states consumers can pick it up but cannot consume it on site. You will need to go through Utah's licensing and training requirements, but the benefits are there isn't any limit to the annual sales amount. Utah is one of the better states for selling homemade food directly to consumers.

# Vermont

**Food and Lodging Program**
foodlodging@vermont.gov
(802) 863-7221
(800) 439-8550

**Vermont Farmer's Market Association**
andrew@nofavt.org
(802) 434 7165

**Vermont Department of Health**
800-439-8550

Vermont is one of the great states that allows homemade hot sauce and spicy foods to be sold directly to consumers through local cottage food laws, but you must file a License Exemption Self-Declaration.

After obtaining licensing you can sell hot sauce and spicy foods almost anywhere, but the only downside is that there is a sales cap of $6,500. If sales exceed $6,500 licensing will need to be obtained from the Vermont Department of Heath.

# Virginia

**Virginia Food Safety and Protection**
**foodsafety@vdacs.virginia.gov**
**(804) 786 3520**

**Virginia Farmers market Association**
**info@vafma.org**

The state of Virginia allows the sale of homemade hot sauce under the Home Kitchen Food Processing Exemption.

However, it can only be sold directly to consumers with a sales cap of $3,000 and sales are not allowed through the internet.

Having no restriction to venues and no licensing requirements still makes the cottage food law a great startup opportunity for hot sauce and spicy food.

# Washington

**State Department of Agriculture**
**cottagefoods@agr.wa.gov**
**(360) 902 1876**

**Washington State Farmers Market Association**
**ben@farmersmarketcoalition.org**

Many states allow acidified foods like hot sauce to be manufactured and sold without following regulations, but Washington is not one of them.

The state approved list provides many of the typical cottage foods like bread, baked goods, and trail mixes.

Following FDA guidelines and getting acquainted with selling hot sauce at a farm market is a perfect opportunity to begin selling elsewhere.

# West Virginia

**West Virginia Department of Agriculture Regulatory and Environmental Affair Division (304) 558 2227**

**West Virginia Farmer's Market Association (304) 398-5214**

Selling hot sauce at a farm market or other temporary location in West Virginia means that you need to follow FDA regulations because all hot sauce is considered non-potentially hazardous regardless of the pH.

If you follow the federal regulations for manufacturing set by the FDA, you can sell anywhere. If you can get hot sauce approved as a shelf stable cottage food, there are no restrictions selling online at markets or stores. However, most farmer's markets like to see locally grown and produced products. West Virgina has a great cottage food law if you are selling spicy foods, snacks, honeys, or spicy jellies.

# Wisconsin

**Wisconsin Farmer's Market Association**
**datcpdfslicensing@wisconsin.gov**
**www.wifarmersmarkets.org**
**(608) 224-4923**

Wisconsin allows the manufacture and sale of hot sauce under the Home Canning Law, but it must include on the label "not subject to state inspections".

Unfortunately selling directly out of your home, through online sales or mail order delivery is not allowed. Wisconsin allows the sale of hot sauce directly to consumers at farm markets only.

However, regulations under the Wisconsin Home Canning Law only allows annuals sales limited to $5,000.

# Wyoming

### Wyoming Department of Agriculture
wda1@wyo.gov
(307) 777 7321

### Wyoming Farmer's Markets
www.wyomingfarmersmarkets.org

Wyoming has become one of the easiest states to sell homemade hot sauce in. Many states since have followed with allowing fermented, acidified and non acidified hot sauce under cottage food law.

All homemade hot sauce needs to be labeled properly stating that it is homemade and does not follow state or governmental inspections. This is typical in many states if you are not following FDA guidelines.

## Setting up

Setting up to sell at a farmer's market will be much different than setting up a store or website. Selling at a farmer's market will set up a temporary store location that will need to be set up and taken down very quickly. Your set up will also need to be designed so that you are able to assemble, disassemble and transport everything.

Setting up a display at a farmer's market should consider two options: paying someone to make the display or putting it together yourself. Setting up a display will have many aspects of marketing associated with it.

## Conclusion

Succeeding at selling a hot sauce at a farm market begins with having a great product, having an available farmer's market where you can sell it, and promoting it face to face with potential customers.

These things can take a lot of work, but many people prove it to be successful...and you can too! No two situations, sauces, state requirements, or farmer's markets are a like so don't get discouraged at the first sign of failure.